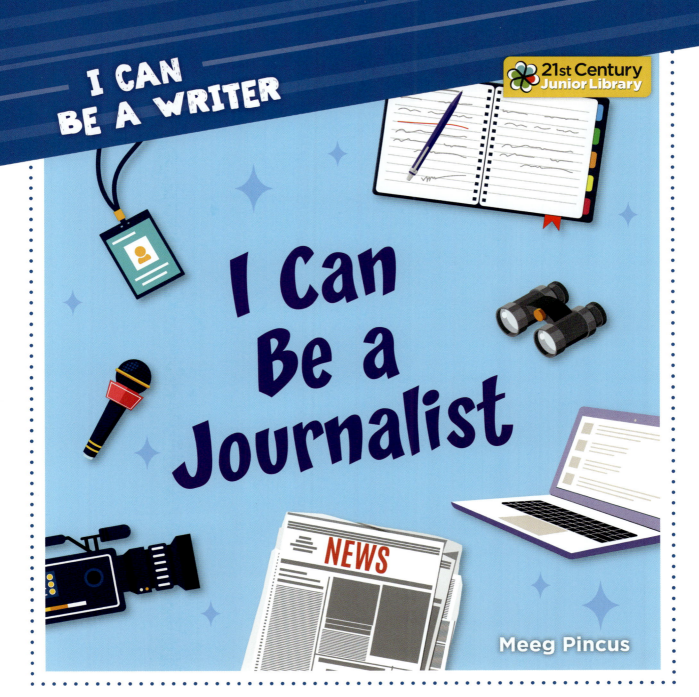

Published in the United States of America by:

CHERRY LAKE PRESS
2395 South Huron Parkway, Suite 200, Ann Arbor, Michigan 48104
www.cherrylakepress.com

Reading Adviser: Beth Walker Gambro, MS, Ed., Reading Consultant, Yorkville, IL

Photo Credits: © Dadann/Shutterstock, 5; © Tsuguliev/Shutterstock, 6; © Pixel-Shot/Shutterstock, 7; © zimmytws/Shutterstock, 9; © Seventyfourimages/Dreamstime.com, 11; © GaudiLab/Shutterstock, 12; © Microgen/Dreamstime.com, 13; © DW labs Incorporated/Shutterstock, 14; © Mircea Moira/Shutterstock, 15; © Aaron of L.A. Photography/Shutterstock, 16; © Wikimedia Commons, Public Domain, 18; © SeventyFour/Shutterstock, 20

Copyright © 2026 by Cherry Lake Publishing Group

All rights reserved. No part of this book may be reproduced or utilized in any form or by any means without written permission from the publisher.

Cherry Lake Press is an imprint of Cherry Lake Publishing Group.

Library of Congress Cataloging-in-Publication Data has been filed and is available at catalog.loc.gov

Cherry Lake Publishing Group would like to acknowledge the work of the Partnership for 21st Century Learning, a Network of Battelle for Kids. Please visit Battelle for Kids online for more information.

Printed in the United States of America

Note from publisher: Websites change regularly, and their future contents are outside of our control. Supervise children when conducting any recommended online searches for extended learning opportunities.

CONTENTS

What Do Journalists Do?	4
Why Would I Want to Write News?	10
How Can I Learn to Write News?	17
Activity	22
Find Out More	23
About the Author	23
Glossary	24
Index	24

WHAT DO JOURNALISTS DO?

Have you ever read a newspaper or news magazine article? Have you watched a **breaking news** story on television? Do you hear people talking about events occurring in the world?

Then you have seen what journalists do!

Journalists investigate and write news—true stories about what's happening in a community.

The first job of a journalist is to find out about any happenings in their **beat**, or the area or topic they cover. They interview people, attend events, and read **documents** to discover news.

Lots of journalists may cover the same event.

Then they use the "Five Ws"—*who*, *what*, *where*, *when*, and *why*—to write news stories. Journalists write for newspapers and news magazines. They also write for television, radio, and online news outlets.

Look!

Notice where people around you get their news. Do they read it, watch it, or listen to it?

Journalists play an important role in a free society. Their job is to report on anything in the **public interest**.

8

Citizens rely on news for truth. They need to know about the governments, businesses, people, and events that affect them. In the United States, news journalism is protected by the **freedom of the press**.

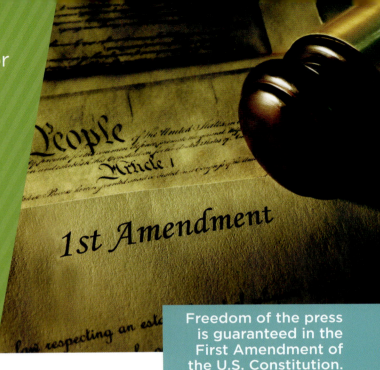

Freedom of the press is guaranteed in the First Amendment of the U.S. Constitution.

Make a Guess!

How do you think news journalists are protected to write the truth? Who protects them?

WHY WOULD I WANT TO WRITE NEWS?

Would you like to make a difference in society? Do you enjoy uncovering facts? Does writing within a set format appeal to you? Does traveling around your community or the world sound exciting? Then you may want to write news!

Journalists check records, files, and other documents to find the truth.

Being a journalist means you're a seeker and writer of true stories and facts. Journalists must be curious and interested in others. They get to meet many diverse people and hear and write their stories.

Do you like the idea of talking with people, searching for documents, and attending events? If so, journalism could be a path for you.

Do you like learning and writing about many new things? As a journalist, you write all kinds of stories.

Depending on your beat, you could write about world news, local news, science, arts, sports—or many of these topics in a given week! A journalist must be a fast learner and a quick writer to report news as it happens.

Ask Questions!

Write a letter to a journalist. Ask why they wanted to write news. Ask what they like most about writing news. Ask anything you're curious about!

Journalists and other members of the press get special access to important events.

Journalists write out questions to ask before an event.

HOW CAN I LEARN TO WRITE NEWS?

News **reporting** has rules you can learn. First are those "Five Ws." You can practice finding out the *who*, *what*, *where*, *when*, and *why* of any news topic.

Try this by attending an event in your community. It could be at the library, city hall, theater, or sports field. Ask people questions or collect documents to gather every *W* about the event. This information gathering comes before writing a news story.

Most Newsworthy Info
Who? What? When? Where? Why? How?

Important Details

Other General Info
Background
Info

Why do you think the most important information comes first?

News is also written in a basic format you can learn. It's called the inverted pyramid or upside-down triangle method. You can practice writing news stories in this format.

The most important and current information always comes first. It's at the top of the upside-down triangle. This is called the **lede** or lead (pronounced "leed").

Other important facts follow the lede. Last comes any background information to help the reader understand the full story. News stories don't have a conclusion, like an essay would.

Create!

Try making a newspaper for your family. You can write stories about family history and what people are doing. Think up a name for it, use pictures, and get creative!

You can take classes in journalism. You can write for your school newspaper. You can even apply to be a news reporter for a kids' news magazine, show, or website.

Can you be a journalist? If you want to investigate and write news stories to inform people about our society . . . yes, you can!

ACTIVITY

Practice finding "The Five Ws" in a news lede. Read the ledes below, and then list the *who*, *what*, *where*, *when* and *why* of each. Here's an example:

Lede: Yesterday, the city mayor visited the Anytown Library to present an award for its outstanding service to residents.

WHO: the city mayor

WHAT: presented an award

WHERE: Anytown Library

WHEN: yesterday

WHY: its outstanding service to residents

Now, you try:

Lede: At Green Field last night, the Anytown Crickets beat the Whoville Grinches to become the regional Little League champions.

Lede: The Anytown Dance Company performed a showcase on Saturday night at the Groovy Theater to kick off its opening season.

FIND OUT MORE

Books

Grant, Joyce. *Can You Believe It?: How to Spot Fake News and Find the Facts.* Toronto, ON: Kids Can Press, 2022.

Holzer, Hannah. *TIME for Kids: Kid Reporter Field Guide.* New York, NY: Penguin Young Readers, 2024.

Websites

With an adult, explore more online with these suggested searches.

"Meet Our Kid Reporters," *Time for Kids*

"What's it like to be a journalist?" video, *School News Network*

ABOUT THE AUTHOR

Meeg Pincus loves to write. She is the author of more than 30 books for children. She has been a writer and editor for books, newspapers, magazines, and more. She also loves to sing, make art, and hang out with her family, friends, and adorable dog.

GLOSSARY

beat (BEET) topic or area that a reporter covers on a regular basis

breaking news (BRAY-king NOOZ) newly received information about an event currently happening

documents (DAH-kyuh-muhntz) written or electronic records that provide information

freedom of the press (FREE-duhm UHV THUH PRESS) right to publish news without government interference

lede (LEED) opening sentence or paragraph of a news story

public interest (PUH-blik IN-tuh-rest) well-being of society as a whole

reporting (rih-POR-ting) gathering and checking facts to present as news

INDEX

activities, 21, 22

beats, 6, 14
breaking news, 4, 5

education, 17, 21
events, 4, 6, 10, 12, 14–16, 17

"Five Ws," 7, 17, 22
freedom of the press, 8–9

inverted pyramid method, 18–19
investigations and research, 4, 6, 10, 12, 16, 17, 21

journalists, 4–9, 10–16, 17, 21, 22

learning, 17–21
ledes, 19

media formats, 4, 7, 21

newsworthiness, 18, 19

press freedom, 8–9
public interest, 8–9

research and investigations, 4, 6, 10, 12, 16, 17, 21

societal role of journalism, 8–9, 10, 12

structures of news writing, 7, 10, 17–19, 22

truth, reporting, 8–9, 10, 12

who, what, where, when, and why, 7, 17, 22
writing news content, 4, 7, 10, 12, 14, 17–19, 21, 22